THEY DON'T BELONG
TRACKING INVASIVE SPECIES

Australia's Cane Toads
Overrun!

by Sneed B. Collard III

Consultant: Rick Shine, AM FAA
School of Biological Sciences
University of Sydney, Australia

BEARPORT
PUBLISHING

New York, New York

Publisher: Kenn Goin
Editorial Director: Natalie Lunis
Senior Editor: Joyce Tavolacci
Creative Director: Spencer Brinker
Design: The Design Lab
Photo Researcher: Jennifer Zeiger

Library of Congress Cataloging-in-Publication Data

Collard, Sneed B., author.
  Australia's Cane toads : overrun! / by Sneed B. Collard III.
     pages cm. — (They don't belong : tracking invasive species)
  Includes bibliographical references and index.
  ISBN 978-1-62724-828-0 (library binding) — ISBN 1-62724-828-5 (library binding)
 1. Bufo marinus—Juvenile literature. 2. Toads—Juvenile literature. 3. Pest introduction—Australia—Juvenile literature. 4. Nonindigenous pests—Australia—Juvenile literature. 5. Nature—Effect of human beings on—Juvenile literature. 6. Australia—Juvenile literature. I. Title.
  QL668.E227C635 2016
  597.8'7—dc23
                                                    2015015252

For more information, write to Bearport Publishing Company, Inc., 45 West 21st Street, Suite 3B, New York, New York 10010. Printed in the United States of America.

10 9 8 7 6 5 4 3 2 1

Contents

A Close Call

In 2013, in the town of Hemmant in northern Australia, Nikita Den Engelse found her dog Wally frothing at the mouth and trembling. "I was concerned he was going to die," she said. Nikita rushed the dachshund-shih tzu mix to a **veterinarian**, who knew exactly what had happened. Wally had been poisoned . . . by a toad.

A dog approaches a toad in northern Australia.

Fortunately, after getting treated by the vet, Wally survived. Many other animals, however, are not so lucky. They die after an experience like this—one that has occurred over and over since an **amphibian** known as the cane toad arrived in Australia.

A cane toad is one of the largest toads in the world. It measures 4 to 9 inches (10 to 23 cm) in length.

Cane toads release poison from their bodies that can make dogs and other animals very sick.

Problem Beetle

Australia's cane toad story began in the 1930s. At that time, Australian sugarcane farmers had a serious beetle problem. Young cane beetles called **grubs** were eating the roots of tall sugarcane plants, causing many plants to die. The farmers tried everything to stop the beetles. They trapped them, poisoned them, and even plucked them off the plants by hand. Yet the cane beetle **population** kept growing.

This is a kind of beetle that attacks sugarcane plants.

Sugarcane is a tall grass that has a stem, or cane, that's filled with sugary juice. In factories, the cane juice is turned into pure white sugar.

In the early 1930s, a team of Australian scientists learned that toads were being used in Hawaii to eat large numbers of cane beetles. In 1935, the scientists went to Hawaii to capture some of the toads. They shipped 102 of them back to Australia with the hope that the toads would kill the plant-destroying beetles in Australia's sugarcane fields.

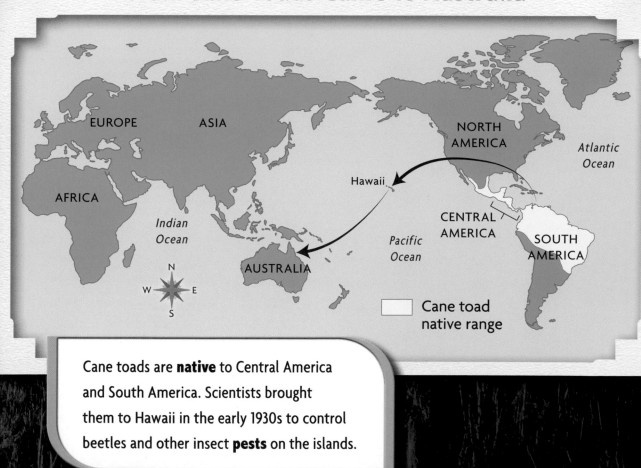

How Cane Toads Came to Australia

EUROPE

ASIA

NORTH AMERICA

Atlantic Ocean

Hawaii

AFRICA

Indian Ocean

CENTRAL AMERICA

Pacific Ocean

SOUTH AMERICA

N
W E
S

AUSTRALIA

Cane toad native range

Cane toads are **native** to Central America and South America. Scientists brought them to Hawaii in the early 1930s to control beetles and other insect **pests** on the islands.

A Failed Experiment

Once in Australia, the toads were kept in **captivity** until they **reproduced**. In several months, scientists had a few thousand baby toads, which they released in the state of Queensland in northern Australia.

By 1938, the toads had become **established** in all of Queensland's sugarcane-growing areas. There was just one problem. The amphibians, called cane toads, weren't doing their job. Why?

A cane toad in a sugarcane field

Cane toads got their name after being used for pest control in Australia's sugarcane fields.

Adult cane beetles often live at the top of tall sugarcane plants. However, cane toads live on the ground—at the base of the plants. Cane toads were not able to jump high enough to reach and eat the beetles. Some scientists hoped the toads would gobble up the beetles after they climbed down the cane plants to **breed**. However, the toads did not eat the beetles on the ground.

Stalks of sugarcane

A cane toad jumps through a field.

Signs of Trouble

The toads didn't just fail to solve the beetle problem in northern Australia. Soon, they were causing problems themselves. As the toads spread out to find food, they ended up in people's backyards. Scientists began receiving reports of poisoned pets. When a dog or other animal grabbed a toad in its mouth, it didn't get a meal. Instead, it became very sick—and sometimes died.

Australia has no native toads.

Cane toads in a backyard in Australia

Parents grew concerned that their children might pick up the toads or even put them in their mouths. People were also becoming more and more worried about the ever-increasing number of cane toads in northern Australia. Unfortunately, it was too late to stop the big amphibians. They had become an **invasive species**.

Fortunately, no children in Australia have died from close contact with cane toads.

Worldwide, there are about 500 species of toads. All of them are poisonous, but few are as dangerous as the cane toad.

Toad Overload

By 1940, there were tens of thousands of toads hopping across northern Australia. One reason this happened is that the toads multiply quickly. Like most amphibians, cane toads lay their eggs in water. For a female cane toad, almost any wet place will do—from a large lake or pond to a small puddle.

Cane toads lay their eggs in long strings. Each string can be 3 feet (0.9 m) long and contain thousands of jelly-like eggs.

Strings of cane toad eggs

Once a mother toad has found a watery spot, she can lay up to 30,000 eggs at a time! Cane toads can also lay eggs up to two times per year. Many of the eggs are eaten by other animals and never hatch into **tadpoles**. However, thousands do survive—and then go on to grow into huge adult toads.

Tadpoles can turn into young toads, called toadlets, in as little as 15 days. These toadlets are ready to leave the water and start living on land.

Eating Everything

Another reason that the number of cane toads skyrocketed is that the toads can eat almost anything that will fit in their big mouths. Their main **prey** are insects, including flies. However, they will eat much larger animals, too. They easily gulp down mice, bats, snakes, and even other cane toads!

This cane toad is eating a smaller toad.

The toads are also very good at tracking down food. Once they left Queensland's sugarcane fields, the toads discovered that by waiting beneath streetlamps in towns, they could grab an easy meal. That's because many night-flying insects are attracted to light and fall or land on the ground underneath the lamps, making it easy for the toads to snatch them up.

Pet food is a favorite meal of cane toads.

a dead kangaroo

These cane toads are feeding on baby flies called maggots near a dead kangaroo.

Toxic Toads

What makes the cane toad especially dangerous to other animals is its powerful poison. Most of the poison is stored in two large **glands**, or sacs, behind the animal's eyes. The milky white poison can also be found in the toad's skin and in other body parts.

poison

When a cane toad is grabbed or attacked, white poison oozes or squirts from the glands behind its eyes.

In the toad's native **habitats**, there are plenty of animals that can safely eat the big amphibian. Over time, these **predators** have become **resistant** to the toad's poison. That isn't true in Australia, however. Because there are no native species of toads there, most predators have never developed resistance to toad poison. For some animals, a single bite of a cane toad can be deadly.

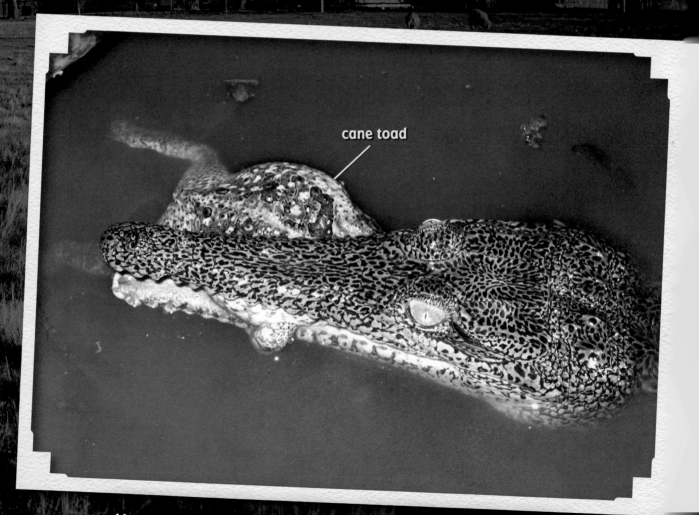

cane toad

Many native Australian predators, such as this freshwater crocodile, mistake poisonous toads for harmless frogs and die as a result.

Conquering a Continent

With its powerful poison and few natural predators, nothing could stop the cane toad from multiplying and spreading beyond Queensland. In just a few decades, the toads numbered in the millions—and they **inhabited** a big part of Australia.

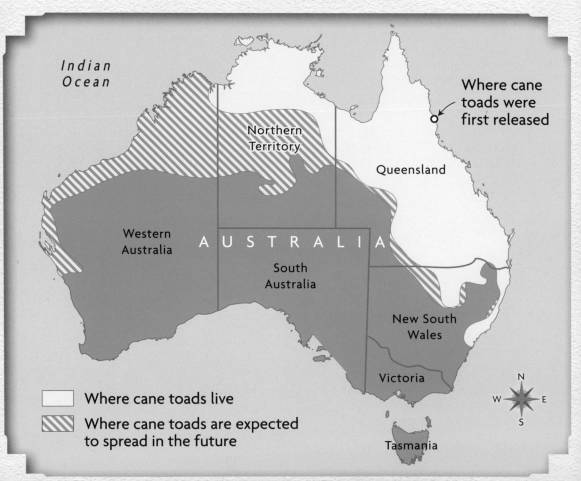

Cane Toads in Australia

Indian Ocean

Where cane toads were first released

Northern Territory

Queensland

Western Australia

AUSTRALIA

South Australia

New South Wales

Victoria

N
W   E
S

Where cane toads live

Where cane toads are expected to spread in the future

Tasmania

Scientists predict that cane toads will spread to many other parts of Australia in the coming years.

Today, the areas in Australia where the toads live cover more than 200,000 square miles (517,998 sq km). That's an area almost the size of Texas. Experts estimate that there may be 2 billion cane toads in Australia—or about 85 toads for each person!

A researcher examines and weighs a cane toad she has captured.

Cane toads can hop faster and farther than other kinds of toads. In Australia, some groups of cane toads have hopped a distance of 37 miles (60 km) per year!

What About Wildlife?

The toad invasion is having a huge impact on many of Australia's native wild animals. Many kinds of predators that eat the toads, including lizards, snakes, and freshwater crocodiles, are dying in large numbers from the toads' poison.

Many lizards, such as the Mertens' water monitor (above), have died after eating a cane toad.

Scientists are especially worried about the deaths of **marsupial mammals**, such as quolls. These small, spotted animals live only in Australia and are very rare. After the introduction of cane toads, the number of quolls decreased because of the marsupials' appetite for the deadly toads.

A quoll is about the size of a cat.

Like all marsupials, quolls give birth to live babies that are not fully formed. The tiny babies finish growing inside their mother's pouch.

A cane toad

Living with Toads

Worried about the possible **extinction** of Australia's quolls, scientists are trying out some unusual ways to save them. Biologist Rick Shine and his team have created "toad sausages." The sausages, which smell and taste like actual cane toads, contain a drug that makes the quolls feel sick but does not kill them. So, by eating the sausages, some quolls have learned to avoid eating live toads.

A blue-tongued skink

Scientists are also using "toad meatballs," made of ground-up toad meat, to train lizards called blue-tongued skinks to avoid eating cane toads.

Other animals are finding ways to deal with cane toads on their own. When the toads first arrived in an area where small marsupials called planigales live, the planigales attacked them. Because planigales are tiny, they only hunted the smallest toads, which have much less poison than larger toads. The small amount of poison did not kill the marsupials, but it made them ill. Just like the quolls, the planigales then learned to stay away from the dangerous toads.

Over time, planigales learned not to eat cane toads.

Crows in Australia have learned how to eat only the less poisonous parts of cane toads.

Can They Be Stopped?

Unfortunately, it might not be possible to teach all predators to avoid cane toads. So scientists are investigating other ways to control them. One way is to remove human-made ponds where the toads often lay their eggs. However, no one can be sure if a plan like this will work.

Because the land is dry in parts of Australia, ranchers often create ponds to provide water for their cattle.

Rick Shine is working on a more promising method. He's using a chemical in cane toad poison to **lure** cane toad tadpoles into traps in places where the amphibians breed. "A chemical **bait** created from the toads' poison is a real magnet for toad tadpoles," according to Shine. So far, the plan is working. "In one natural pond, we collected more than 40,000 toad tadpoles in less than a week," he said.

Biologist Rick Shine with a cane toad

The chemical bait used by Shine attracts only cane toad tadpoles. The bait **repels** other animals, such as native frogs and fish.

After the tadpoles are trapped, they are killed.

Lessons Learned

People created the cane toad problem. However, it's not too late to learn from the mistake and work toward fixing it. As a way to prevent the spread of invasive species, Australia has created tough laws to keep other harmful pests out, which has inspired other countries to do the same. Ordinary Australians are also helping out in the war against toads.

A bucketful of captured cane toads

Many Australians **volunteer** to catch and kill cane toads in order to help control their numbers. Other people have built toad-proof fences around their yards. By working together, people and scientists can help protect native wildlife and stop this amphibian invader from spreading to new areas.

A cane toad by a swimming pool

After volunteers catch the toads, they **humanely** kill them.

Fences have helped keep cane toads out of people's backyards and away from their pets.

Other Invasive Amphibians

Here are three other invasive amphibians that are causing problems around the world.

African Clawed Frog

- African clawed frogs come from cool parts of central Africa. They grow up to 5 inches (13 cm) long—that's about the size of a human hand.

- African clawed frogs are used as lab animals and make popular pets. As a result, they have been shipped all over the world. Some frogs escaped into the wild, while others were released by their owners into ponds, rivers, and lakes.

- Today, the frogs live in North America, South America, and Europe. They multiply quickly and eat many native fish and frogs.

American Bullfrog

- American bullfrogs are native to the eastern United States. They can grow up to 10 inches (25 cm) long.

- Bullfrogs were brought to California in 1898. Why? People there wanted to use the frogs' legs as food. Since then, the frogs have been introduced to Asia, Europe, and South America.

- Like cane toads, bullfrogs breed rapidly. They eat many other animals, including **endangered** amphibians.

- American bullfrogs carry a deadly disease that can harm other amphibians. The disease may have already caused the extinction of dozens of species around the world.

Coqui Frog

- Around 1988, coqui frogs were accidentally introduced to Hawaii from Puerto Rico. They are now found on four different Hawaiian Islands.

- Coquis are small frogs that are about the size of a quarter. They make loud, high-pitched calls.

- Up to 36,000 coquis can live in a single acre of Hawaiian forest.

- A group of 30,000 coquis can eat up to 250,000 insects and other small animals in a single night.

- Coqui frogs have no natural predators in Hawaii.

Glossary

amphibian (am-FIB-ee-uhn) an animal that lives part of its life in water and part on land

bait (BAYT) food used to attract an animal to a trap

breed (BREED) to produce young

captivity (kap-TIV-uh-tee) a place where an animal lives that is not its natural home and where it cannot travel freely

endangered (en-DAYN-jurd) in danger of dying out

established (ess-TAB-lishd) settled in an area

extinction (ek-STINGKT-shuhn) when a type of animal has died out

glands (GLANDZ) body parts that produce natural chemicals, such as poison

grubs (GRUHBZ) the worm-like form of young beetles

habitats (HAB-uh-*tats*) places in the wild where animals normally live

humanely (hyoo-MAYN-lee) done in a kind, gentle, and caring manner

inhabited (in-HAB-it-id) having lived in or occupied a place

invasive species (in-VAY-siv SPEE-sheez) a kind of animal or plant from somewhere else that can cause harm in its new home

lure (LOOR) to attract

marsupial mammals (mar-SOO-pee-uhl MAM-uhlz) a group of animals, which includes opossums and kangaroos, that carry their babies in pouches

native (NAY-tiv) animals that are born in and spend their lives in a particular place

pests (PESTS) animals that cause damage or other kinds of problems

population (*pop*-yuh-LAY-shuhn) the total number of a kind of animal living in a place

predators (PRED-uh-turz) animals that hunt and kill other animals for food

prey (PRAY) animals that are hunted and eaten by other animals

repels (ri-PELZ) pushes away

reproduced (*ree*-pruh-DOOSD) had offspring

resistant (ri-ZIS-tuhnt) the state of not being affected by something, such as a disease or poison

tadpoles (TAD-pohlz) small, young frogs or toads that lack legs and live in water before they become adults

veterinarian (vet-ur-uh-NER-ee-uhn) a doctor who cares for animals

volunteer (*vol*-uhn-TIHR) to do a job without pay

Bibliography

Lewis, Stephanie. *Cane Toads: An Unnatural History*. New York: Doubleday (1989).

Llewelyn, John, et al. "Behavioural responses of carnivorous marsupials (*Planigale maculata*) to toxic invasive cane toads (*Bufo marinus*)." *Austral Ecology*, Vol. 35, 560–567 (2010).

Shanmuganathan, T., et al. "Biological control of the cane toad in Australia: a review." *Animal Conservation*, Vol. 13, Suppl. 1, 16–23 (2010).

Read More

Collard, Sneed B., III. *Science Warriors: The Battle Against Invasive Species (Scientists in the Field)*. Boston: Houghton Mifflin (2008).

Gray, Leon. *Cane Toad: The World's Biggest Toad (Even More Supersized!)*. New York: Bearport (2013).

Seibert, Patricia. *Toad Overload: A True Tale of Nature Knocked off Balance in Australia*. Brookfield, CT: Millbrook (1996).

Learn More Online

To learn more about cane toads in Australia, visit
www.bearportpublishing.com/TheyDontBelong

Index

About the Author

Sneed B. Collard III has written more than 70 books for young people. In 2006, he received the prestigious *Washington Post* Children's Book Guild Nonfiction Award for his body of work. Visit him at www.sneedbcollardiii.com.